My Autobiography

Barbara Henning

OTHER BOOKS BY BARBARA HENNING

Smoking in the Twilight Bar
Love Makes Thinking Dark
In Between
Me & My Dog
Black Lace
Detective Sentences
You, Me and the Insects

MY AUTOBIOGRAPHY

Barbara Henning

UNITED ARTISTS BOOKS 2007

My Autobiography was previously published as a limited edition in 2004 without the notes and in a slightly different version. Some of the poems were published in *Shiny*. Special thanks to Paul Klinger, Chris Tysh, Lewis Warsh and Rodney Phillips for help with editing and proofreading.

Author's Note:

This poem grew out of a collaboration with the artist Miranda Maher. Miranda clipped off the corner of 999 of my books for an installation, entitled 999. Then I constructed the poem by taking a word, a phrase, or passage or two from each of these books, using alliteration as the knot between the lines, and allowing myself the freedom to end and begin each line where I wanted, often letting the alliteration fall away, but leaving the natural rhythm that either preceded or followed the sound. Most of the time, I made minimal changes. Sometimes I rearranged the lines. The surprise was that many of the poems took shape without much revision; one line seemed to effortlessly find its partner in the next book, from Agee, Artaud and Apollinaire to Zukofsky and all the way into the kitchen to my cookbooks.

Cover and book design by Miranda Maher
www.mirandamaher.com

Author photograph: Dondi Tondro

First Edition
ISBN: 0-935992-43-X

United Artists Books
114 W. 16th Street, 5C
New York, NY 10011
www.unitedartistsbooks.com

for Louis Zukofsky

1

We shall wish to see the houses
I saw a fine street whose name

like the blessed bread at mass
had an existence of its own

your great grey retains
like a vibrating nut

for the journey, my brother
you do not sleep at night

so if we die before dawn
nothing ever happens

the dirt around the geraniums
just jungles really and daytime

domestic scenes, picturesque
old fashioned pumps market a nod

2

beneath this accumulation
of nailed boots cut down uproot

I happened on a photograph
of Napoleon's brother

released in Paris in mid-october 1931
one means is employed, now another

admirer of war contracts
among architecture, magazines, recycled

fools only themselves
the conclusion, it had all been

burning until all that hate
it may change us also

a sort of attraction for images
so it is with the lover at grips with figures

3

fifteen days left I think
in the softness of the woods

such a truth is negative and we will not
now on this corner

contemplate with dazed astonishment
a flower on a grave

guillotined, she had a head of her own
oh for us wretched old females

faire un monceau de voeux
a simple book, if you insist

constantly on the run from creditors
rises and sails and banks of sod

colors on a canvas, Marie stretched
crepuscular, bluish shot with rose

4

one is tempted to add as a postscript
color slides of the warm climates

perhaps its hard brown crust
kamikakazes mixed

moon poppies backdrop
billions. Of course it also explains why

the baboons have all been dead for ages
a sentence says you know

the middle ground of care in particulars
requires a firm wham of the fingers

family finances, everything but desire
it always struck me as a bit ludicrous

later I learned that he was only twenty
take off your head; un-loose your duck

5

downcast . . . the slob beside her
he wants to be a brutal old man

man, men, maul her body
blasphemy! someone's got

a pointed beard—he saw this. He
hath found, all outward loathing

how had he come to be here
a leaf, a feeling of light

to learn, in harvest to take
a cake of virgin's wax

whether on Ida's shady brow
or on the beautiful but awe inspiring

cold winter wind bringing with it
a word Blake used carelessly

6

crumbling griffins and shameless
babylonic cries

come here little dear
during the last few months

duende has become associated
with catalogs, crimes with no dead bodies

air flames on her skin
true we would not dare venture

serenely in the sunshine to sigh
Sal we miss her, Maum Sal

so what if he isn't one of the stung
returning to our mammal brothers

seventeen years later I sit down
on a rock overlooking the sea

since number five is out of the bathroom
no. it was an accident

a unique aesthetic
alas, we are stuck

in the insane asylum
of misunderstandings

where the unfolding of
one day I can't say when

wealth will rock down against us
and we will throw out our

supple and strong bodies
just to pay for our books and tuition

there are many junk pyramids
today I embark on instructions to become a catholic

coming of the big red
chalky swallow

six feet wide and eight feet high
during the day

your ex-friend changes his name
now and then a car slows down

his eyes and cheeks bathed
below bobble dents and speed bumps

were not side view mirrors our hosts
when her hair gets in her way

descending is deceptive
day blazed and now approaches

adding four new row houses
pyramids like pavement

verb plunged and stone tacked
a pond in a tree

towing him around and around
leafless whipped the vague air

as if tomorrow and tomorrow
with tiny cups inside the palms

of his hands, a ball-bearing company
coils strapped to his back

he had the respectable interest
but by his own ineptness

all a rhythm, remembering
the figure by the window

while there's still time, Thomas
you're considered the least dispensable

down wall from girder into
laughter and shadows

cavernous halls for eating
otherwise on a stairway

even cold then
the sidewalks are narrow

nothing because everything
while the slippery eyes

decoy an organized following
for many days he wouldn't leave

the world of spirits
still life bizarre apparitions

the mirth in the mail of anguish
one day I find myself

11

and time yet for a hundred
others who have claimed

pray gather me, anemone
inmost in due time becomes the outmost

for each ecstatic instant
all human beings think of the self

or of the ell added ca1835
I think it sad to have a friend

for whom I robbed the dingle
not disorder, order is not

a neophyte in full entrance
even in bed, I thought

they'd all say you're a lovely
lumpy disproportionate person

and now friend, I do not know
if I put some sugar on the fruit

far as I know, no, never
not the dereliction or the flowing

as fast as a wind raging
ravished and ravaged with desire

dans une pension d'état a Saigon
the simultaneous order

speaks only as though
wedges of light flap

from wharf to ant farm
five peeled treetrunks

at times I feel like a man
meaning something slightly different

divagations autour d'une oeuvre
I'll put a period in your head

Hassan, we found you on the GW
but I tell you a cat needs a name

neither plentitude nor vacancy. Only
OOOO that Shakespherian

right of reason made a freeman
else to-morrow a stranger will say

suffering a severe nervous breakdown
and B.O. I sweated too much

the meat packer who always ate
brewing wild tea on the domestic

grass to make the light beneath
colchicums around which dragons fly

14

he drags his bare feet
flog alpenglow with a rubber hose

first we had a couple of feelers
father's hands never left the keys

critics and anthologists busy themselves
with the first version, that of 1926

in the commune of Aunay, a fearful murder
and the ancient temple over which it was built

it would be a mistake to suppose
the spirit is visiting this time

to melt and be like a running brook
to sob and then many sobs

the rhythm the rhythm—and your memory
these intellectual golden threads

bazaar stalls round and round
but empty body. So that there is

neither modest nor immodest
smackdabbed

into the luminescent night
get up and get out or

hand me down those blasting caps
I remember when St Marks

was a male. A tradition. The sixties
I feel that I may never talk much

occasional reveries
rollover and remember to replace

ravenous the still dark a fishnet
for clarity which is not about access

another home game
to push one foot ahead of another

I'm hung on remembering
Helen gazing at her husband

did I think of him as Mercury
as grapes in the "goblets"

as ugly and little to be desired as
a round lamp made of blue glass

for we have found you
seven days and I have not seen her

he seems instinctively to have snapped
back and hung over his slippery

intellectual curiosity
reaching an all-time peak in 1914

fatherland freedom & at the bottom
you were right the first time

before the collector gets off
five thousand, three hundred and twenty nine

bodhidharma's fierce, bushy brow
time to stave off disaster change

now he bobs like my toy plastic bird
only the dull make no response

on the sidewalk with her boyfriend
pass my crossing like shadows

she stays here, considers, and just to take up
the complications of the present

damn that kid, uncle George says
strolling down second avenue at midnight

sure, losing is a hard word
as they are spoken

true in those days I did not
go to poetry readings to find love

let's bring it to a close
conversion to copy

couldn't even say Jack Robinson
ropes and stripes, black and white

sun and moon, no herb
helium balloons spill off the horizon

he told me all love doesn't end in tragedy
to speak of love until they lose it

I John bright picture
passionate lines at the oakem

a book, and particularly a first book
one of her favorite authors

and fences—their eyes are ancient
beat back into the blood—

so I write as one speaks to one's shadow
slaves working in the hot sun

shells exploding around a man and in his flesh
"be well runt" and what's the fuss

over a layered lookalike
the drawing of a house, penciled by a child

trembling like the traffic. I am on the back
of the chicken truck then in the tangle

awake, believing that she is beautiful
betty byrne lived; she sold lemon platt

pinched it out of the skivvy's room
read: July 1, 1985

a few harsh words to loosen the pen
plurality is all. I walk among the restaurants

and recent luncheon guests at the broadway
boxing gloves. I have written

with wings of gentle flush o'er delicate
woodruff is gone

gone forever, even the sweet
sound is part of the physical quality

required in every line, not a like or an as
but a few bees come in with ashen mouths

and melancholic psychomotor retardation
on the rainy highway, his words still in his mouth

the most awful of beings
me? the cop? certainly not.

the ruling conventions might come to impose
I must first introduce myself

not the sensation of not knowing
but nursing dependence would seem to exhibit

y'all though seem to be drowning in a puddle
a pattern of rushing away to escape

New York City, its stacked hybrid ways
endearing to us our tongues

we cast ourselves adrift on the ocean
collecting jars along its curve

on the one hand it's the idea
on the other a map of creation

at the gold vase of kings
keep the book for as long as you like

smoking cigarettes and watching
keys jingle in the door ajar, threatening

the greyness of marching men
Mina Loy was fairly hard on herself

to wear the temporal raw
an upholstered contraption tied with slipknots

her mother was one of the many women
who recoil and then repeat

round russets
the russian word pravoslavniy

the prick containing forged material
in fall of 1975, nineteen years old

23

only a child!
chez tous broutant

blue clouds touch off an emotion
of round and round for years

you gave yourself to others, but
suddenly veer or wind and rain

rough and deep as the bed of torrents
today the governess in order that Madame's

eyes will cast a shadow on her outward
Oliver's shrinking elbow, Oliver

on the pavement of my trampled soul
somebody who wants them to shine a bit

but mama's sick in bed
and Billy Bodega doesn't like it

he leans against the machine, reels, &
I'll make you a bet on alert mountain top

the snow, you forget. They're coming
to get a beer, carrying twins

meddling though I'd still like to do it
as secret as mummies the wild psychoanalysts

then conjoin to see the sights of Avenue C
smooth liquor, Stumpy MacPhail

strangely chiming a song identical
with the air, bewitched by the loveliness

sometimes we'll abhor it and shut our eyes
as a way to end wars

the sight of Lycidas who charms the young
experience: your awareness of experience

To uncover once we've fled
with my pointed tongue

as the prime mover of exports
Ezra Pound clearly stands out

temporarily composed in the chevy
you took us for carnation ice cream

such a bum when I finally did get pregnant—
he called me pessimistic

his wife sofia and their son were still living
what happened between us is (not)

a rite that was once practiced
or a notion of racial hierarchy or exclusion

pues la sancta inquisicion suele ser tan diligente
a city like this one makes me dream tall

she's very old and dirty, whistling her filthy
dark river beds down

don't shoot the rail
or the rivers in prayer like monasteries

"money will not" "be enough" "a woman"
what can it do like this

the cinema a cruel Miracle
moon you're the candid the lucent

heavily natured town where we heard
the other day at the guggenheim

gossip about her having shown up drunk
he is also a monkey there

dressed in a plain white T-shirt
likewise, rapture can be a form of detritus

heart-shorn, lip-sick, breath-weary
totally uncharacteristic of modern poetry

dogtown, scattered
paste-board masks of moby-dick

truth is, I don't think he cared
what I damn well fall back to

the goodness in her? And what was the cost?
a closed car—closed in glass

currents and storms had taken away
a sort of summer hard budges blossom

but we imagine others
as still and quiet, the angel of knowledge

with no space-time coordinates
I am, by the way, celebrating the city of my birth

born December 27, 1910
to be alive is to be a great noise

no man could swim in air, no man could breathe
but— this much you can do—give in as if

you're a beatup mercedes
maybe it's my age, prime of life, you know

no, no, I am not mentioned
with the print of a million moving feet

fear would deface & topple
finish up as a jackal's lunch

a butterfly through the window
walking back up the street, momentarily

mother's voice now full of irritation
I mean I would sort of appear

columbia application came today
tap, tap, tap, steel pegs

at four a.m. the cars down the block were shells
she had grown up with her mother

her passions, from that hapless hour
were far more intolerable than it had seemed

pumped ahead by these pistons, this blood
brought home to me by our next door neighbor

Norton opened his eyes; they stung
symptomatic of the unsettling specificity

of the Poe-etic effect, three quotations
from one of the oldest and most respectable

a multitude of books came in for review
radical, a primitive impulse—elementary

earnest longing for artificial excitement
electrified by the weird cry of

now and then, did my spirit fully
keep at least one of my promises

in the place of the springs
where she stops to tie her shoe

she had always leased to foreigners
five other poems appeared

and she whom you seek
still working at his forehead with her thumb

this dogfish was probably unconscious
unbroken by the sumoon

such a pain desire had wrought
WHATSOEVER on his habitually slack attention

they both become pupils of Buddha
I don't care a fried _____about nationality

what's normal, makes him ab-normal
again, however, a significant

nay! for I have seen the purplest shadows
Sieburth writes, "the text is rather a jigsaw

a petition: AGAINST Europes and Xtiantity
candid (he was talking) less than

a devil with a pail full of grapes
the kidney that was the original site

he had been ravished up into a fiery cloud
car son Pegase qui rue

who can know there was a child weeping
you've got the front darling—

why don't you try a little harder
his poor mother gives mikythos' picture

to a background of dots in a series
synanon made a therapeutic method out of

a hundred pages, mostly very affectionate
against a conspiracy of silence

struggling with opening of part V
vespasian or his son and the meanest

flower beds were later set up
under the sheets and blankets

I leaned my head on his shoulder
a for sure cigar smoking jazz and blues

with little distraction beyond conversation
picture after picture in the egyptian books

when the going is gone
and the games they forbade

the modern literary background
decide if it is sensible

indeed they were neither
it says and does not say

green. And we have been riding
large-written catchwords

though never a complete wipe out
a crusade, unrecorded voyages of

damask damning languorously
those solemn energetic

diversions of princes
facing it, that is, still facing away

34

otherwise set the stage
mindlessly by the low but mighty

manhattan. It is too late
little magazines survive

smash through their coverings
the winter snow like toilet paper

plump little cupid digs
for you beautiful ones

unfortunately, afterthoughts are
as one might hide a stone in grass

girl spat on when she has boy "push"
peaceful – time – we're in it – or near it

in your open angle and melodious thighs
they are as good as salt

so, either by thy picture or by my love
like prosody in a methodical

invigorated gulf
it'll never work right and everyone knows

Gertrude Stein, who as early as 1911
hath not? Rosalind lacks then

upon our leavings
larger than life, which is interesting

I know what it means, my language
left banares on the kashi express

even bananas with seeds
gain fluency even as they

create wars and pointless loves
little sales ladies little sales ladies little saddles

doesn't make a dent
displaying constellations

made natural and untimely
until with them still

several ways that mothers or fathers
five and no more five and four four and four

at once more than all at once
one formulates until what is to be

better than the opera because it went on
oh yes oh yes

you & I are the formulation we are
and who shall speak it what child or wanderer

without a name and nothing
to catch a broken nap with house rum

who walks against wind growing
rose red with beatings

an ironic fervor
flux though it was cold and windy

leviathan east, largely
light under the roof in the

devil's eyebrows. Standing like a stone figure
for hours the innocent

R. lay down opposite each other
climbing sea from Asia had me down

Ricardo tells me, don't forget yourself
yes, in the middle

madame realism watches his movements
money burns the pocket

Margot, she makes me sick
with the stale atmosphere, reeking of ammonia

as an actor even though he was
what makes you think

the need to compensate for a feeling
factors such as enclosure

the dog of Jean de Nivelle
nothing like that was ever forgotten

or permitted to continue
its episodes carefully

frangipani flamboyant
delicate with little blue mustache

completely contemporary criminal
cleveland or detroit

electricity and answering
all day mother, afraid the cords

cradling bliss
I interrupt with a question

key west. He was born in a suburb of boston
unable to distinguish between waves and corpuscles

in the third cross
there remained of her only a sweet fragrance

for a really hot fire, use bark
because that is what he was

we face great holocausts
he shot this salmon with his 30-30

the room was full of grace
"goose" means "fool" in english

40

O baffled, bulk'd, bent to the very earth
every condition promulges

Emerson was helpless but he accepted
what is commonest, cheapest, nearest, easiest

my mother looked on in delight
DAY 11, the day after my birthday

does the heart have to beat at a super
speed, to write a poem, to pour over one's past

as if a stair at the top of which a DEGREE
don't give them anything instinctively

through the next solar system
someone whose speech

is it a dirty book? I'll bet
babies and I wanted to write about them

steiglitz probably became aware
while he was in town

even when we do get rid of them
that's what we'd all like to be, Bill

and yet one must. But even
I have not slept through

a thousand other places
safe from enemies

and he had to assume
he went to a lot of

sea creatures with human heads
to try to give up smoking

perhaps this fly has no wish
to fall and only then sideways

she helped the soup as if
it is not you that I call unseen, unheard

vitiate it, slay it here. Now
noon and cold night

never shall a young man
hurt   so that none   rule

my uncle was horrified
the recalcitrance of William Carlos Williams

why first pour wine
when a new spirit in that world

walks naked God song of his wood
what comfort of goodness was there

the sense of the first line is clear
clear mirror, care his error

entrenched literary position
agonizing deprivation of junk sickness

from computer to CD-Rom
radically distinct from their work

wonder each time I read
straight ahead and murmur

most of them are poets in their 20's
Eliot's place as the god of the work-shop

shirt-sleeved swede old spits on snow
stiff shudderings shook the heav'nly

confused geography of its beginnings
in non-chronological juxta-position

consisting of an indefinite number
notice how the impression of speed increases

through the eyes of Olson's generation
Guido Cavalcanti has its real center

a scornful, technical masterpiece
the mayor of needles for a couple

restrictive labels. Those earlier designations
soon forgotten

fruit juices and lost audiences
the convention in art ranges

and also places in the universe
this kind of pressure, the lesser writer

when she encounters the fact of herself
Hamlet, nor was ever meant to be

Barbara Henning: "east detroiter" staff 2; pit and
    balcony drama
dorcas, bowling clubs, Ferne Hostetter 3187 alder road.

ribbon, her slender ribbon
Rogers! I who saw their ever film

faultline irreproachable prayers
people's abandonment in that very thing

the white alaskan daisy, yellow marigol
in drivel of accusations, lamentably a capella

craning to see then, slowly
so much of duty as you may require

returned for the second time
toast the buns and ring the bell

but "imagism" was largely "picturism"
containing *i, h, s, c, u, y, a, e, t*. Take positions

public readings have often involved
I could diminish. My title

two: the point at which you read
of the oppressed extremist

even though they collapse into the sea
Snyder and Whalen, the difference

Palmer once said
describing in an unembellished

play of numbers offers the possibility
from conventional pieties

of "past" and "present complicated
Cage's poetry, as about his music

marginalized women have been
rather facilely says Bernstein

stripped of the first layer of skin
startling effects and a major project

parochial society—from slave to citizen
cast their eternal brilliance over the

white man, as a consequence
common melody with which we

wear the familiar signs
the saying goes, the whites were taking over

the crossing sign is, of course, enormous
omitting records of a certain kind

as early as 1957 it was no longer
laughter, the brutal rhythms

of respectability. Nuyorican
equals new poetry: one which is born

breathtakingly elegant long permanent
change. However, I will do what I can

crick crack. The voice tells
took up my mother on my back

brighten the night a little
licked until they have no more

laugh a hag's laugh
through darkness to darkness

dew has faded his ruby lips
the winds that blow—ask

these horses. Among these days
departing spring

since I first made my count
clap sidewise: I am not his yet

yes, churlish heart, it was good
going back to the States. Do you want to?

49

to break up the dancing here
he rescued all those knights

I wonder can this be the world
why this scrambling around so low

life passing in solitude
snow above love above speechless

screaming, General, you are beginning
but since I am not the body

blessed are those who wash their
reward is with me to give every man

mahanama dived into the water and they were
pleased with him, and he with them

the mystery of supreme discipline
dramatically and wildly or simply

50

women have been displaced
spiritual people in this world

directing their concentration
toning the nerves, muscles, organs

our enemy is a paper tiger
to be open is to accept two truths

tal dadara is consisting of eight
even before one proves their excellence

everywhere I exist, yet I am
as long as the prana does not

naturalistic mystics fall into
dire need of the nector

nothing you wish is impossible
in the avenue leading to the water

51

like nirvana or buddhahood
at each conquered height

he who can give me
more than ten several times

desireable as it is
to conquer the subtle passions

an internal contradiction
clad with zeal as a cloak

clumsy, awkward, absurd
unfortunate these minor figures

so near to the age of the sage
with no food or drink

a pain in my back becomes
corpses of large birds, corpses of small birds

osiris. Bless this body
burn the prayer mat

more prestige, more power
some of these left over

produces a certain degree
of deceptive existence

for years, however, this vast
virtue takes charge

on farsightedness
firmly place the legs

lie down and rest for five
foreign dominating powers

mighty stone foot of the statue
a problem? Nobody tells us

suddenly horizontal reveals
Richard. Anywhere. He's here

everything depends upon what
Hanuman and Sugreeva and all the

respiratory organs, breathing
reality, only a snake knows a snake

and all the trees of the field
making the compound grove radiant

as earth, he would always be there
the good old sage

seat yourself on a clean spot
some say they saw it

if one wants to express
mother is present in every house

literation, literator, literature
letter. A written monologue

monometer. A line of verse
has this been heard by you, Arjuna?

arouse the kundalini energy
getting back to normal

the independent sovereign pope
never in one's life

P'u: unwrought simplicity
in stanzas of eight or more

leisure. The real problem
polish poetry has its beginnings

in brood. Progeny, offspring, young
you had to step over three or four

middle summit of mongaup mountain
minor damage to shore facilities

formerly indifferent countries, like england
examined in isolation

interpretation of
frescoes and ceilings, that as a leading

leader, hunter and fisherman
fight with Moses

one thousand nine hundred and sixty nine years
yes. Thank you

the train, the bed, the field
finally, the last drawings

are darker and the lights lighter
let's pick up the pace a bit, sir

see how it is possible
to reproduce lace-like sculpture

between her knees
Singh inscribed the miniature

mclough steel filed for bankruptcy
no more than marginal

Marsh's fabric, opined
plagued by a rising crime rate

oh please don't go
because that country is on the eve

of the paradox of dada
each is equally possible

divorced from a truly creative
lucidity at Bro's. Friday it started

stamps were fabricated
frank as ever, but their sexual urgency

unfinished, notably
in the neighborhood Andrea explored

earlier, he had made
some of Duchamp's own

oh miserable of happy. Is this the end?
exhibited along with lithographs

the landscape of my country
Cain's jealousy of Abel

a bed, her head cast downward
with deep respect for the other

witchcraft, the evil was
new explorations into experimental

empty room confronted by
nothing very new

I think I have read everything of
hele helele the king is a great king

Matta and Gordon Onslow Ford are still
an analemma, showing by inspection

not our concern for the time being
by reason not of merit of their own

oedipus complex which in turn is
naturalism that had begun to make

mountain landscape by 1980
eureka, eureka, or that the law of inverse

society shares the assumption
an end to the burden of shame

she retained a memory
of the woman. Such is God

a cover for his own novel
not a struggle to the death

to these should be added
skepticism is correct

such impurities as remain
found in our woods and fields

wavering tests of our conceptions
a wedge of late sunlight

duchamp's most disturbing ideas
as cries, shouts and bursts

literary language—it is
an umbrella on a dissecting table

conquer England. An impressive moment
(identifiable by the net) around his

human experience metaphorized
without going or coming

characteristic curves
unless it doesn't take the first

desire for artistic expression
forcing the majority, whom

wake up or time to die
which the public may comprehend

as completion in citation
but which cannot be digested

double triangle 1966 acrylic on
civilization, India never separated

poor young william
to whom do these

louver a gap
guns, other infantry, still

stars in search of the
sheer lechery you were

whatever your age
blue lines concur

as if I'm becoming
air fire man beast

reverberations. pools
memory at 4 a.m.

an idea of birds
of water, of wind

our creator foresaw the wretched
whilst they were doing

therapy they would be
likely to develop coronary

and who are less
aspiring to stop the pain

with chronic kidney
don't lick or shape the ends

against leeches
lye, gasoline, or a pesticide

into the bottom of a well
they suffer from depression

dip a banana in a piece of waxed paper
the worms should come up

under two handfuls
the leftovers can be stored

in a soup pot
in same sit with knees drawn

growing and eating them
a dense coat of short villous

pastry hairs. It is ideal
if there is a family history

of pignoli nuts: also called
a high altitude area facing

standardization seems to be slowing
the history of the great yogi

scrub well and cut out
yo followers yo quilters yo pushcarts

pillowed in your arm, a blue
borderless. homespun soaked

more than a flapping flatfish
fabio glides across la stanza

still you have died three times
you've learned a trade—

strangers now, but once we were lovers
in a real sense

a sanction. I must warn you
we have had the occasion

one was alive, one was dead
drifting toward the empire's end

the excitement it generated
around us. With these beginnings

but to survey all the people
parliamo italiano language school

sapphires of work and study
sir, why? Because whatever

worldly pleasures to the other shore
under the influence of

occupation la profesión
I knew you had a problem

every piece composition
couldn't be too much

men were like kings
malcolm coming its true

turtles love on a heavy afternoon
when abundance leads to contentment

completely wrapped up
to possess him like ghosts

grits or gardenias or call him
to tilt their ashen horizon

written with the idea of publishing
parts uncertain in the end, right?

back from a wave
it will be from me to you

you'll brim with social graces
say goodbye even in a letter

I woke up with your name
linoleum, black and white

I needed you? The boar
both distinct, side by side

to bring in the raspberry
freedom in unseen waters

whirlpool awe indecorous
I need a beer and a cognac

council resolution 1325 makes our case
Cliff, we talk about women

water drains out of the coconut
constituting the inner process

yet its quality is sattvic
a sore throat caused by

breeding within the corpse
within them all

a trait often missing in the leaders
laugh has hasati

68

here in this world
it is indeed our good fortune

to spread out in this wide
finite subject

translating his golden threads
turning his heart

hence the name
from that country scanty

struck by its peculiar look
the world unknown

under the bodhi tree
think about it. It is

written at the request
of rituals and musical performances

would you like to play
pictures framed at angles

probably none of
the winter months have passed

toward the double locked
legs, closed to catch the falling

yet another perspective
and they were right

dancing this way with
the tonic or postural

problems inseparable from
fantastically complicated

cardboard folders with flaps and black clothes
Cardullo's sold bay leaves and cloves

Koko remains motionless
motorboats around here are out

to leave a place so quiet
quickly swing it open. The road

rich with greenery as
in mysterious forms like gods

gaining entry, to spread out
only one thing matters now

needles of pine brilliantly
bombarding them with stones

so many local customs can
crash them to the ground

govern is the will
to talk in whispers

the poem reads, don't obey
the status of muslim women

he finally relented
and will be calling the faithful

friend to his final
re-moulding nearer

to the heart's apologies
a feat which the quran

comes silently and takes thy
sand rising on the outskirts

one would have to trust
traveling. He was of the light

low people. I've heard that—
today, where are all the dark paths

through it all, Yudhistra
went out in the hot sun

the infinite pilgrimage
obstacles we have gone through

with paper, separate and inside
figures ducking carelessly

on the threads of midnight
an indispensable sea

it's an old experience
a tall birth appearing

sideways increasing error
darling, the salt rum

can barely project the title
in this house experimental

Notes

Each poem is composed of fourteen lines; there is a note for each line. If one line was derived from more than one book, the titles are separated with semicolons. There is some alphabetic sense in the beginning, but then as we go along, the list is as scattered as my books.

1

James Agee	Let Us Now Praise Famous Men
Guillaume Apollinaire	Alcools
Guillaume Apollinaire	The Poet Assassinated
Antonin Artaud	Selected Writings
James Agee	Collected Poems
Kathy Acker	Blood and Guts in High School
Alvin Aubert	Against the Blues
Yehuda Amichai	Amen
Ai	Cruelty
Anna Akhmatova	Poems
John Ashbery	The Tennis Court Oath
John Ashbery	Self Portrait in a Convex Mirror
Walter Abish	In the Future Perfect
Rae Armantrout	Precedence

2

James Baldwin	The Evidence of Things Not Seen
Kathy Acker	Great Expectations
Roland Barthes	Camera Lucida
Roland Barthes	Camera Lucida
Steven Barber	Antonin Artaud
Aristotle	The Poetics
David Lehman	Beyond Amazement
John Ashbery	Can You Hear, Bird
John Ashbery	Houseboat Days
John Ashbery	April Galleons
John Ashbery	Rivers and Mountains
Margaret Atwood	The Journals of Susanna Moodie
Gaston Bachelard	The Poetics of Space
Roland Barthes	A Lover's Discourse

3

Georges Bataille	The Tears of Eros
Georges Bataille	The Dead Man
Georges Bataille	Theory of Religion
Georges Bataille	Story of the Eye
Leo Bersani	Baudelaire and Freud
Charles Baudelaire	Intimate Journals
Georges Poulet	Baudelaire, the Artist and his World
Charles Baudelaire	Twenty Prose poems
De Boisoeffre	La Poésie Française de Baudelaire à Nos Jours
Jean-Paul Sartre	Baudelaire
Pascal Pia	Baudelaire
Charles Baudelaire	Flowers of Evil
Charles Baudelaire	Selected Writings on Art and Literature
Charles Baudelaire	Paris Spleen

4

Margery Evans	Baudelaire and Intertextuality
Charles Baxter	Imaginary Paintings
Charles Baxter	The South Dakota Guidebook
Paul Beatty	Big Bank Takes Little Bank
Martine Bellen	10 Greek Poems
Michael Benedikt	Night Cries
Kenneth Bernard	The Baboon in the Nightclub
Charles Bernstein	Content's Dream
Charles Bernstein	A Poetics
Anne Waldman	Nice to See You: Homage to Ted Berrigan
Ed Foster	Code of the West: Memoir of Ted Berrigan
Aaron Fischer	Ted Berrigan: An Annotated Checklist
Ron Padgett	Ted: Personal Memoir of Ted Berrigan
Ted Berrigan	A Certain Slant of Sunlight

5

John Berryman	The Dream Songs
Robert Creeley	Mirrors
Robert Creeley	A Day book

Aloysius Bertrand	Flemish School, Old Paris, & Night & Its Spells
Aloysius Bertrand; Frank Bidart	Flemish School, Old Paris, & Night & Its Spells; The Sacrifice
John Donne and William Blake	Complete Poetry & Selected Prose
Elizabeth Bishop	Geography III
Mei-mei Berssenbrugge	Four Year Old Girl
William Blake	The Marriage of Heaven and Hell
Geoffrey Keynes	The Letters of William Blake
Alfred Kazin	The Portable Blake
Kathleen Raine	Blake and Antiquity
Charlotte Brontë	Jane Eyre
S. Foster Damon	A Blake Dictionary

6

Emily Brontë	Wuthering Heights
Djuna Barnes	The Book of Repulsive Women
Charlotte Brontë	Villette
Maurice Blanchot	Death Sentence
Robert Bly	Leaping Poetry
Alicia Borinsky	Timorous Women
Mei-Mei Berssenbrugge and Kiki Smith	Endocrinology
André Breton	Manifestoes of Surrealism
Elizabeth Browning	Sonnets from the Portuguese
Sterling Brown	Collected Poems
Terrance Malley	Richard Brautigan
Richard Brautigan	The Pill Versus the Spring Hill Mining Disaster
Richard Brautigan	Trout Fishing in America
Nicole Brossard	Picture Theory

7

Gwendolyn Brooks	Blacks
Esther Broner	A Weave of Women
Gwendolyn Brooks	A Life Distilled
Lee Ann Brown	Miss Traduction
Cleaneth Brooks	The Well Wrought Urn

Paul Buck   No Title
Paul Buck   Walking into Myself
Paul Buck   Naming Names
Charles Bukowski   The Days Run Away Like Wild Horses
                             Over the Hills
Charles Bukowski   The Most Beautiful Woman in Town
William Burroughs   Queer
William Burroughs   Naked Lunch
Charlotte Carter   Personal Effects

8

Blaise Cendrars   Complete Poems
William Corbett   Lift Magazine Corbett Issue
William Burroughs   My Education, a Book of Dreams
Mary Ann Cameron   Heartwise in Detroit
Peter Bushyeager   Mute Dog
Raymond Carver   What We Talk About When We Talk About
                             Love
Blaise Cendrars   Sky Memoirs
Abigail Child   Mob
Paul Celan   Poems
Raymond Carver   Cathedral
Hélène Cixous   Three Steps on the Ladder of Writing
Paul Claudel   A Hundred Movements for a Fan
Norma Cole   Moira
Wanda Coleman   Heavy Daughter Blues

9

Samuel Taylor Coleridge The Rime of the Ancient Mariner
Clark Coolidge   Own Face
Dennis Cooper   The Tenderness of Wolves
William Corbett   Columbus Square Journal
Cid Corman   Nothing At All
Brenda Coultas   Early Films
Kelly Craig   Gulf Coast IV, 2
Lynn Crawford   Blow
Robert Creeley   Niagara Frontier Review
Robert Creeley   For Love
Robert Creeley   Words

Robert Creeley	Collected Poems
Robert Creeley	Life & Death
Vincent Quinn	Hart Crane

10

Hart Crane	Complete Poems
Hart Crane	The Bridge
Lynn Crawford	Solow
Stella Crews	Thieves or the Laundromat Bandit
Victor Hernadez Cruz	Snaps
E. E. Cummings	Magic-Maker
E. E. Cummings	Six Nonlectures
E. E. Cummings	Is 5
Don David	The Limitation of Soiling
Lydia Davis	Sketches for a Life of Wassily
Fielding Dawson	Three Penny Lane
Lydia Davis; Fielding Dawson	Almost No Memory; Three Penny Lane
Emily Dickinson	Poems
Gerard de Nerval	Aurelia

11

T.S. Eliot	The Waste Land and Other Poems
Ralph Waldo Emerson	A Collection of Critical Essays
Emily Dickinson	Selected Poems & Letters
Ralph Waldo Emerson	Self-Reliance and Other Essays
Emily Dickinson	Final Harvest
Cynthia Griffin Wolff	Emily Dickinson
Polly Longsworth	The World of Emily Dickinson
Emily Dickinson	New Poems
Emily Dickinson	Selected Poems
Robert Duncan	The Opening of the Field
Robert Duncan	Bending the Bow
Diane di Prima	Memoirs of a Beatnik
Diane di Prima	Pieces of a Song
Diane di Prima	Dinners and Nightmares

12

Diane di Prima	Loba
Rachel Blau DuPlessis	The Pink Guitar
Marguerite Duras	L'amante Anglaise
Rackstraw Downes	Under the Gowanus and Razor-Wire Journal
Marguerite Duras	The Lover
Marguerite Duras	The Ravishing of Lol Stein
Marguerite Duras	L'amant
T.S. Eliot	Selected Prose
Allen Tate	TS Eliot: The Man and His Work
Elaine Equi	Decoy
Elaine Equi	Surface Tension
Elke Erb	Mountains in Berlin
Elaine Equi	Friendship with Things
Theodore Enslin	Conversations

13

Louis Parrot	Paul Eluard
George Economou	Ameriki Ameripikh
George Economou	Landed Natures
T.S. Eliot	Old Possum's Book of Practical Cats
T.S. Eliot	Four Quartets
T.S. Eliot	The Waste Land and Other Poems
Swami Paramananda	Emerson and Vedanta
Ralph Waldo Emerson	Essays
Carlos Baker	Emerson Among the Eccentrics
Lawrence Ferlinghetti	Her
Joe Brainard	I Rcmember
Ian Hamilton Finlay	Chapman
Allen Fisher	Scram
Robert Desnos	Night of Loveless Nights

14

Allen Ginsberg	Reality Sandwiches
Allen Ginsberg	Poems for the Nation
T.S. Eliot	The Wasteland, a Facsimile
Edward Foster	The Angelus Bell
Edward Foster	Answerable to None

Michel Foucault	This is Not a Pipe
Michel Foucault	I, Pierre Rivière, Having Slaughtered My Mother, My Sister, and My Brother
Sigmund Freud	Civilization and Its Discontents
Sigmund Freud	The Interpretation Of Dreams
Amy Gerstler	Nerve Storm
Khalil Gibran	The Prophet
Allen Ginsberg	Composed on the Tongue
Allen Ginsberg	Kaddish
Allen Ginsberg	Howl

15

Allen Ginsberg	Indian Journals
Allen Ginsberg	Allen Verbatim
Allen Ginsberg	Howl Original Draft Facsimile
Joshua Beckman	Object Lesson: Poetry Machines
Larry Gabriel	Dreams Swing Daily
Barbara Greene and Bob McTaggart	Cages
Michael Gizzi	Interferon
John Godfrey	Midnight on Your Left
Paul Green	The Polidori Perfection
John Godfrey	Dabble
Paul Green	A Comparative Daimon
Barbara Greene and Bob McTaggart	Poems from the City of Light
Barbara Guest	Defensive Rapture
Paul Green	Communicator

16

Phillip Good	Corn
Barbara Guest	The Blue Stairs
Bobbie Louise Hawkins	Almost Everything
Homer	The Odyssey
H.D.	Tribute to Freud
H.D.	Signets H.D.
H.D.	Notes on Thought and Vision
Deborah King	H.D. Woman and Poet
H.D.	Collected Poems 1912-1944

Ezra Pound and Noel Stock	Love Poems of Ancient Egypt
H.D.	End to Torment
H.D.	The Gift
Barbara Guest	Herself Defined
Thomas Burnett Swann	The Classical World of H.D.

17

Robert Hale	Vexillum
Yukihede Hartman	New Poems
Carla Harryman	There Never Was a Rose Without a Thorn
Carla Harryman	Memory Play
Sam Hamill	Mandala
Michael Heller	Wordflow
Lyn Hejinian	My Life
Lyn Hejinian	Happily
Barbara Henning	Black Lace
Lolita Hernandez	Snakecrossing
Barbara Henning	Smoking in the Twilight Bar
Barbara Henning	Love Makes Thinking Dark
Ernest Hemingway	The Nick Adams Stories
Mitch Highfill	Liquid Affairs

18

Edward Hirsch	For the Sleep Walkers
Bob Holman	Panic DJ
Friedrich Hölderlin and Eduard Morike	Selected Poems
Bell Hooks	Wounds of Passion
Lita Hornick	Great Queens Who Loved Poetry
Richard Howard	Untitled Subjects
Fanny Howe	Eggs
Fanny Howe	The Deep North
Fanny Howe	O'clock
Fanny Howe	The End
Fanny Howe	Saving History
Fanny Howe	Introduction to the World
Susan Howe	The Nonconformist's Memorial
Fanny Howe	Robeson Street

19

Steven Tracy	Langston Hughes and the Blues
Susan Howe	My Emily Dickinson
Susan Howe	The Europe of Trusts
Langston Hughes	Selected Poems
Edmond Jabès	The Book of Questions II
Langston Hughes	Collected Poems
Edmond Jabès	The Book of Questions I
Lisa Jarnot, Bill Luoma and Rod Smith	New Mannerist Tricycle
Jarnot, Luoma and Smith; Yang Jiang	New Mannerist Tricycle; Six Chapters from My Life Down Under
Lisa Jarnot	Ring of Fire
Lisa Jarnot	Sea Lyrics
Lisa Jarnot	Some Other Kind of Mission
Randall Jarrell	The Complete Poems
James Joyce	A Portrait of the Artist as a Young Man

20

James Joyce	Ulysses
James Joyce	Dubliners
Garrett Kalleberg	Limbic Odes
Weldon Kees	The Collected Poems
Robert Knoll	Weldon Kees and the Midcentury Generation
John Keats	Selected Letters
John Keats	Poetical Works
Malcolm King	Identity
Galway Kinnell	The Avenue Bearing the Initial of Christ into the New World
Kenneth Koch	Making Your Own Days
Kenneth Koch	Wishes, Lies and Dreams
Daniel Krakauer	Poems for the Whole Family
Julia Kristeva	Black Sun
Bill Kushner	He Dreams of Waters

21

Bill Kushner	Love Uncut
Bill Kushner	Head
Jacques Lacan	Feminine Sexuality
Jacques Lacan	The Four Fundamental Concepts of Psycho-analysis
Joanne Kyger	Strange Big Moon
Jacques Lacan	Ecrits
The Last Poets	Vibes from the Scribes
Ann Lauterbach	Clamor
Gary Lenhart	One at a Time
Gary Lenhart	Light Heart
Denise Levertov	Light up the Cave
Kimberly Lyons	Abracadabra
Denise Levertov	The Poet in the World
Philip Levine	One for the Rose

22

Andrew Levy	Democracy Assemblages
Clarice Lispector	Selected Cronicas
Gerald Locklin	A Constituency of Dunces
Audre Lorde	Our Dead Behind Us
Mina Loy	The Lost Lunar Baedeker
Virginia Kouidis	Mina Loy
Kimberly Lyons	In Padua
Colleen Lookingbill	Incognita
Carolyn Burke	Becoming Modern
Robert Lowell	Selected Poems
Bill Luoma	Ode
Elizabeth MacKiernan	Ancestors Maybe
Jackson Mac Low	The Virginia Woolf Poems
Jackson Mac Low	Crayon

23

Stephane Mallarmé	A Tomb for Anatole
Stephane Mallarmé	Poems
Bernadette Mayer	Another Smashed Pinecone
Dennis Moritz	Something to Hold On To

Jim Marsh	Again in Complete Steel
Mao Tse-Tung	Poems
Tommaso Marinetti	Selected Writings
Edgar Masters	The New Spoon River
Harry Mathews	Armenian Papers
Harry Mathews	Cigarettes
Vladimir Mayakovsky	Poems
Vladimir Mayakovsky	How Are Verses Made?
Vladimir Mayakovsky	The Bedbug
Harry Mathews	20 Lines a Day

24

Bernadette Mayer	Memory
Bernadette Mayer	Two Haloed Mourners
Bernadette Mayer	The Golden Book of Words
Bernadette Mayer	Proper Name
Bernadette Mayer	The Desires of Mothers to Please Others in Letters
Bernadette Mayer	Bernadette Mayer Reader
Bernadette Mayer	Sonnets
Carson McCullers	The Ballad of the Sad Café
Duncan McNaughton	Valparaiso
Herman Melville	Pierre or the Ambiguities
Bernadette Mayer	Midwinter Day
Bernadette Mayer	The Ethics of Sleep
Bernadette Mayer	The Formal Field of Kissing
Harry Mathews	Immeasurable Distances

25

Jennifer Moxley	Imagination Verses
Joyce Mansour	Screams
Mark McMorris	Moth-Wings
Patricia Willis	Marianne Moore: Vision into Verse
Wendy Mulford	The East Anglia Sequence
Harryette Mullen	Tree Tall Woman
Charles Cantalupo and Barbara Mor	Poetry, Mysticism, and Feminism
Harryette Mullen	Muse & Drudge
Vladamir Nabokov	Glory

Laura Moriarty	Spicer's City
Laura Mullen	The Tales of Horror
Toni Morrison	Playing in the Dark
Susan Nash	Mind Noir & El Siglo de Oro
Toni Morrison	Jazz

26

Frank O'Hara	Lunch Poems
Pablo Neruda and Cesar Vallejo	Selected Poems
Lorine Niedecker	The Granite Pail
Pablo Neruda	Let the Rail Splitter Awake
Alice Notley and Douglas Oliver	The Scarlet Cabinet
Alice Notley	Close to Me & Closer
Frank O'Hara	Selected Poems
Alice Notley	Songs for the Unborn Second Baby
Alice Notley	Selected Poems
Frank O'Hara	Art Chronicles 1954-1966
Brad Gooch	City Poet
Alice Notley	Margaret & Dusty
Marjorie Perloff	Frank O'Hara: Poet Among Painters
Claire Needell	Not a Balancing Act

27

Frank O'Hara	Early Writing
Robert Von Hallberg	Charles Olson, Scholar's Art
Charles Olson	Poetry and Truth
George F. Butterick	A Guide to the Maximus Poems of Charles Olson
Charles Olson	The Post Office
George F. Butterick	Olson & Creeley: Complete Correspondence
Tillie Olsen	Tell Me a Riddle
George Oppen	Collected Poems
Charles Olson	Call Me Ishmael
George Oppen	This in Which
George Oppen	Of Being Numerous
George Oppen	The Materials

Tom Clark	Charles Olson: The Allegory of a Poet's Life
Charles Olson	Reading at Berkeley

28

Charles Olson	Selected Writings
Maureen Owen	Big Deal 5
Ovid	Metamorphoses
Ovid	The Art of Love
Gary Pacernick	Something Is Happening
Grace Paley	Later the Same Day
Grace Paley	The Little Disturbances of Man
Kenneth Patchen	Collected Poems
Kenneth Patchen	Hallelujah Anyway
Georges Perec	A Void
Fernando Pessoa	Poems
Simon Pettet	Selected Poems
Wang Ping	American Visa
Jayne Anne Phillips	Black Tickets

29

Sylvia Plath	Letters Home
Sylvia Plath	Collected Poems
Jayne Anne Phillips	Counting
Jayne Anne Phillips	Fast Lanes
Edgar Allan Poe	Complete Poetry & Selected Criticism
Edgar Allan Poe	The Narrative of Arthur Gordon Pym
Sylvia Plath	Ariel
Sylvia Plath	The Bell Jar
Sylvia Plath	Johnny Panic and the Bible of Dreams
John Muller; Jacqueline Rose	The Purloined Poe; The Haunting of Sylvia Plath
Muller and Richardson	The Purloined Poe
Warren Ober	The Enigma of Poe
W. Bittner	Poe
Edgar Allan Poe	Short Fiction

30

Raymond Foye	The Unknown Poe
Kenneth Silverman	Poe, Mournful and Neverending Remembrance
Edgar Allan Poe and Charles Baudelaire	Seven Tales
Maria Jose de Lancastre and Antonio Tabucchi	Fernando Pessoa
Francis Ponge	The Making of the Pre
Anthony Petrosky	Jurgas Petraskas
Mary de Rachewiltz	Ezra Pound, Father and Teacher: Discretions
James Longenbach	Stone Cottage
Ezra Pound	The Confucian Odes
Charles Olson	Charles Olson & Ezra Pound
Ezra Pound	Guide to Kulchur
Ezra Pound	Selected Poems
Ezra Pound	Confucius to Cummings
Ezra Pound	ABC of Reading

31

Hugh Kenner	The Translations of Ezra Pound
D. D. Paige	The Letters of Ezra Pound
Charles Norman	The Case of Ezra Pound
George Bornstein	Ezra Pound Among the Poets
Ezra Pound	Collected Early Poems of Ezra Pound
James Laughlin	Pound as Wuz
Ezra Pound	The Cantos of Ezra Pound
Stephen Ratcliffe	Private
Kristin Prevallet	The Parasite Poems
David Rattray	How I Became One of the Invisible
David Rattray	Opening the Eyelid
D. Noakes	Raymond Radiguet
Pierre Reverdy	Roof Slates and Other Poems
Michael Price	Doombook

32

Kenneth Rexroth	Collected Shorter Poems
Kenneth Rexroth	Poems from the Greek Anthology

Kenneth Rexroth	The Collected Longer Poems
Kenneth Rexroth	The Alternative Society
Kenneth Rexroth	Assays
Kenneth Rexroth	Bird in the Bush
Linda Hamalian	A Life of Kenneth Rexroth
Charles Reznikoff	Complete Poems
Charles Reznikoff	Holocaust
Jean Rhys	Complete Novels
René Ricard	Trusty Sarcophagus Co.
Kenneth Wheeler	Out of Brooklyn
Deborah Baker	In Extremis: The Life of Laura Riding
Laura Jackson Riding	The Word Woman

33

Laura Jackson Riding	Selected Poems in Five Sets
Arthur Rimbaud	Complete Works
Laura Jackson Riding	The Telling
Laura Jackson Riding	Four Unposted Letters to Catherine
Laura Jackson Riding	Progress of Stories
Laura Jackson Riding	Selected Poems in Five Sets
Rainer Marie Rilke	The Lay of the Love And Death of Cornet Christopher
Rainer Marie Rilke	Wartime Letters
Jerome Rothenberg	Pre-Faces & Other Writings
Arthur Rimbaud	Season In Hell and the Drunken Boat
Arthur Rimbaud	Illuminations
René Ricard	God with Revolver
Arthur Rimbaud	Complete Works
Alain Robbe-Grillet	Snapshots

34

Jerome Rothenberg	Revolution of the Word
Raymond Roussel	Selections from Certain of his Books
Douglas Rothschild	Christmas Card
Muriel Rukeyser	The Life of Poetry
Mowlana Jalaluddin Rumi	Like This
Michah Saperstein	Two Cows in Love
Joan DeJean	Fictions of Sappho
Diane Rayor	Sappho's Lyre

Tom Savage	Political Conditions/Physical States
James Schuyler	Freely Espousing
Leslie Scalapino and Kevin Killian	Stone Marmalade
Leslie Scalapino	Goya's L.A.
Leopold Senghor	Collected Poetry
Anne Sexton	The Death Notebooks

35

William Shakespeare	The Sonnets
Karl Shapiro	Essay on Rime
David Shapiro	The Page-Turner
Hal Sirowitz	No More Birthdays
Ron Silliman	The New Sentence
William Shakespeare	Complete Signet Classic Shakespeare
W. D. Snodgrass	Heart's Needle
David Snow	The Cafe Review, Vol. 5
Gary Snyder	Regarding Wave
Gary Snyder	Passage Through India
Gary Snyder	Left out in the Rain
Juliana Spahr	Testimony
Jack Spicer	Collected Books
Gertrude Stein	Tender Buttons

36

Sor Juana	Sor Juana Anthology
Robert Spector	Love Poems & Others
Richard Kostelanetz	The Yale Gertrude Stein
Gertrude Stein	How to Write
Gertrude Stein	Blood on the Dining-room Floor
Gertrude Stein	Lucy Church Amiably
Gertrude Stein	Stanzas In Meditation
Lew Welch	How I Read Gertrude Stein
Gertrude Stein	Lectures in America
Gertrude Stein	The Geographical History of America
Harris Schiff	In the Heart of the Empire
Wallace Stevens	The Necessary Angel
Wallace Stevens	The Palm at the End of The Mind
Dennis Teichman	Edge to Edge

37

Chris Tysh	In the Name
Alfred Tennyson	Idylls of the King
Tod Thilleman	A World of Nothing but Nations
Henry David Thoreau	Cape Cod
Chris Tysh	Coat of Arms
George Tysh	Ovals
Dylan Thomas	Portrait of the Artist as a Young Dog
Dylan Thomas	Quite Early One Morning
Steve Tudor	Tudor's Anatomy
Dylan Thomas	Collected Poems
Lorenzo Thomas	There Are Witnesses
Lynne Tillman	Cast Masks in Doubt
Lynne Tillman	Madame Realism
Jean Toomer	Cane

38

Lewis Warsh	The Maharajah's Son
Lewis Warsh	Agnes & Sally
Lewis Warsh	Private Agenda
Lewis Warsh	Part of my History
Lewis Warsh	A Free Man
Lewis Warsh	Methods of Birth Control
Paul Verlaine	Selected Poems
Ian Taylor	Ruins
George Tysh	Echolalia
Tristan Tzara	Seven Dada Manifestos and Lempisteries
Anne Waldman	Iovis
Anne Waldman	Blue Mosque
Diane Wakoski	The Motorcycle Betrayal Poems
Anne Waldman	Fast Speaking Woman

39

Lewis Warsh	Dreaming as One
Lewis Warsh	The Corset
Diane Ward	Human Ceiling
Rosemarie Waldrop	The Reproduction of Profiles
Lewis Warsh	Money Under the Table

Rosemarie Waldrop	Lawn of Excluded Middle
Keith Waldrop	The Space of Half an Hour
Robert Walser	Masquerade and Other Stories
Lew Welch	Ring of Bone
Aram Saroyan	Genesis Angels
Lew Welch	How I Work as a Poet
Lew Welch	Selected Poems
Nathanial West	Miss Lonelyhearts & the Day of the Locust
Phillip Whalen	Every Day

40

Walt Whitman	Walt Whitman's Poems
Walt Whitman	Leaves of Grass
Wilson Allen	The Solitary Singer
Geoffrey Sill	Walt Whitman of Mickle Street
Walt Whitman	Poetry and Prose
Hannah Weiner	The Fast
John Wieners	Journal of John Wieners is to Be Called 707 Scott Street for Billie Holiday 1959
John Wieners	Selected Poems
William Carlos Williams	Collected Poems Volume 1
William Carlos Williams	Collected Poems Volume 2
William Carlos Williams	Imaginations
Gary Lenhart	Teachers & Writers Guide to W.C. Williams
William Carlos Williams	Paterson
William Carlos Williams	I Wanted to Write a Poem

41

B. Dijkstra	Cubism, Stieglitz and the Early Poetry of William Carlos Williams
Jane Wodening	The Book of Legends
William Carlos Williams	The Farmers' Daughters
William Carlos Williams	Asphodel,That Greeny Flower and Other Love Poems
William Carlos Williams	Selected Essays
William Carlos Williams	Pictures from Brueghel and Other Poems
Diane Ward	Never Without One
Jeanette Winterson	Written on the Body

James Breslin — William Carlos Williams
Jane Wodening — The Book of Legends
Elizabeth Willis — The Human Abstract
Terrance Winch — Total Strangers
Tyrone Williams — Convalescence
Tyrone Williams — Callaloo, 22.1

42

Virginia Woolf — To the Lighthouse
Walt Whitman — Leaves of Grass
C.D. Wright — Just Whistle
Richard Wright — Haiku- This Other World
William Butler Yeats — Selected Poems and Two Plays
Louis Zukofsky — Autobiography
William Butler Yeats — The Autobiography of William Butler Yeats
Louis Zukofsky — Prepositions
Louis Zukofsky — All
Louis Zukofsky — A Test of Poetry
Louis Zukofsky — A
Louis Zukofsky — Ferdinand
Barry Ahearn — Zukofsky's A
Louis Zukofsky — Complete Short Poetry

43

Seymour Krim — The Beats
Donald Allen
    and Robert Creeley — New American Story
Jerome Rothenberg
    and Pierre Joris — Poems for the Millenium, Volume II
Paris Leary and Robert Kelly — A Controversy Of Poets
Dougles Messerli — Gertrude Stein Awards in Innovative
    American Poetry

Amy Scholder
    and Ira Silverberg — High Risk
Paul Carroll — The Young American Poets
Andrei Codrescu — Up Late: American Poetry Since 1970
Tom Clark — All Stars
William Blake — America a Prophecy, Stonybrook 3/4
Emmett Williams — Anthology of Concrete Poetry

Jerome Rothenberg and George Quasha	America a Prophecy: A New Reading of American Poetry
Stephen Kuusisto, Deborah Tall and David Weiss	The Poet's Notebook
G. Leech	A Linguistic Guide to English Poetry

44

Donald Allen and Warren Tallman	The Poetics of the New American Poetry
M.L. Rosenthal	The New Poets
J.D. McClatchy	Poets On Painters
Edward Foster	Postmodern Poetry: Talisman Interviews
Donald Allen and George F. Butterick	Postmoderns: The New American Poetry Revised
Tom Clark	The Poetry Beat
Anne Waldman and Marilyn Webb	Talking Poetics from Naropa Institute 1
David Perkins	A History of Modern Poetry
Anne Waldman and Marilyn Webb	Talking Poetics from Naropa Institute 2
Jeanette Winterson	Art [Objects]
Suzanne Juhasz	Naked and Fiery Forms: Modern American Poetry By Women
Barbara Herrnstein-Smith	Poetic Closure
East Detroit High School	East Detroiter (Yearbook 1966)
Northeastern High School	Northeastern High School Aryan 1939

45

Harryette Mullen	Trimmings
Bill Kushner	That April
Chris Tysh	Continuity Girl
Leslie Scalapino	Crowd and not Evening Or Light
Steven Schreiner	Imposing Presence
Michael Scholnick	Clinch
James Scully	Avenue of the Americas
Edna St. Vincent Millay	Fatal Interview
Sappho	Poems & Fragments

Nathalie Sarraute	Tropisms
Robert Bly	American Poetry
Bruce Andrews and Charles Bernstein	Language Book
Ron Silliman	In the American Tree
Douglas Messerli	Language Poetries

46

Bob Perelman	The Marginalization of Poetry
James Scully	Line Break
James Breslin	From Modern to Contemporary
Kenneth Rexroth	American Poetry in the Twentieth Century
Lisa Jarnot, Leonard Schwartz and Chris Stroffolino	An Anthology of New (American) Poets
Leonard Schwartz, Joseph Donahue and Ed Foster	Primary Trouble
Marjorie Perloff	The Futurist Movement
Juliana Spahr and Mark Wallace	A Poetics of Criticism
Marjorie Perloff	Wittgenstein's Ladder
Marjorie Perloff	Radical Artifice
Marjorie Perloff	Poetic License
Poetics Journal	The Person
Warren Motte	Oulipo: A Primer of Potential Literature
Harry Mathews and Alastair Brotchie	Oulipo Compendium

47

Leroi Jones	Blues People
Franz Fanon	Black Skin White Masks
Jean Wagner	Black Poets of the US
Ellen Kennedy	The Negritude Poets
Houston Baker	Modernism and the Harlem Renaissance
Julio Finn	The Bluesman
Houston Baker	Blues, Ideology, and Afro-American Literature
Arna Bontemps	American Negro Poetry

Paul Oliver, Max Harrison,
   and William Bolcom   The New Grove: Gospel, Blues and Jazz
Sascha Feinsein and
   Yusef Komunyakaa   The Jazz Poetry Anthology
Miguel Algarin
   and Miguel Piñero   Nuyorican Poetry
Alfred Matilla
   and Ivan Silen   The Puerto Rican Poets
Lorenzo Thomas   Extraordinary Measures
Gaye Brown   The Dial: Arts and Letters in the 1920s

48

Aldon Lynn Nielsen   Black Chant
Stephen Carter   Traditional Japanese Poetry
Abdullah Ul-udhari   Modern Poetry of the Arab World
Makoto Ueda   Modern Japanese Tanka
Kenneth Rexroth
   and Ikuto Atsumi   Women Poets of Japan
Ono no Komachi
   and Izumi Shikibu   The Ink Dark Moon
Kenneth Rexroth
   and Ling Chung   Women Poets of China
Harold Gould Henderson   An Introduction to Haiku
Octavio Paz, Jacques
   Roubaud and
   Edoardo Sanguineti   Renga: A Chain of Poems
Robert Hass   The Essential Haiku
Harriet Monroe   The New Poetry
Gerald Sanders
   and John Nelson   Chief Modern Poets of Britian
                                 and America
Gwendolen Murphy   The Modern Poet
Donald Hall   Remembering Poets

49

Paul Blackburn   Proensa: Troubadour Poetry
Magda Bogin
   and Meg Bogin   The Women Troubadours
Robert Bain   Whitman's & Dickinson's Contemporaries

Colin Wilson	Poetry & Mysticism
John High	The Desire Notebooks
John High, Vitaly Chernetsky, et al	Crossing Centuries: Russian Poetry
Leroi Jones	The Moderns
David Godman and Ramana Maharshi	The Teachings of Sri Ramana Maharshi
Standard Revised Version	The Holy Bible
Authorized Version	The New Testament
Japan Kyokai	The Teaching of Buddha
Everyman's	The Koran
Barbara Stoler Miller	The Bhagavad-Gita
Ron Padgett	Handbook of Poetic Forms

50

Elizabeth Bumiller	May You Be The Mother of a Hundred Sons
B.K.S. Iyengar	The Tree of Yoga
Swami Saraswati	Backward Bending Asanas
Swami Saraswati	Moola Bandha
Peter Wilson and Bill Weinberg	Avant Gardening
T.K.V. Desikachar	Health, Healing & Beyond
Sadashiva of Mysore	Notebook: Tablas Lessons
Daniels Ingalls	Sanskrit Poetry
Mahendra Nath Gupta	The Gospel of Sri Ramakrishna
Pancham Singh	The Hatha Yoga Pradipika
K.T. Behanan	Yoga: a Scientific Evaluation
George Feuerstein	The Shambhala Guide to Yoga
Stephen Mitchell	The Book of Job
David Rosenberg	A Poet's Bible

51

W.Y. Evens-Wentz	Tibetan Yoga
Luc Venet Satprem	Sri Aurobindo the Adventure of Consciousness
Paul Brunton	Discover Yourself
Sacan Bercovitch	The Puritan Origins of the American Self
George Feuerstein	Tantra

Mahatma Gandhi	Autobiography
Thomas Merton	Zen And the Birds of Appetite
King James Version	Concordance to the Holy Bible
Marcia Nardi and	
William Carlos Williams	The Last Word
Umesh Patri	Hindu Scriptures and American Transcendentalists
Betty Radice	Mencius
Burton Watson	The Lotus Sutra
John Sarno	Healing Back Pain
Thich Nhat Hanh	Love in Action

52

Normandi Ellis	Awakening Osiris: Egyptian Book of The Dead
Ainslee Embree	Sources Of Indian Tradition
J. Krishnamurti	On Fear
Confucius	The Analects
Daisetz Suzuki	Zen and Japanese Culture
Carole Tomkinson	Big Sky Mind
Jean Varenne	Yoga and the Hindu Tradition
Lao-Tzu	Tao Te Ching
Aldous Huxley	The Art of Seeing
Andre Lappa	Yoga: Tradition of Unification
Sri K. Patthabi Jois	Yoga Mala
N.E. Sjoman	The Yoga Tradition of the Mysore Palace
William Dalrymple	Sacred India
U.G. Krishnamurti	The Courage to Stand Alone

53

Gloria Frym	Homeless at Home
Dennis Barone	Echoes
Mircea Eliade	Yoga Immortality and Freedom
R. K. Narayan	Ramayana
Rammurti S. Mishra	The Textbook of Yoga Psychology
Sri Swami Satchidanada	The Yoga Sutras of Patanjali
Paramahansa Yogananda	Autobiography of a Yogi
Paul Brunton	A Search in Secret India
Chogyam Trungpa	Cutting Through Spiritual Materialism

Sir Richard Burton	The Kama Sutra
Frederick Manchester and	
Swami Prabhanananda	The Upanishads
A.K. Ramanujan	Speaking of Siva
Ajit Mookerjee	Kundalini
Heinrich Robert Zimmer	Philosophies of India

54

Rosalin Ferguson	Rhyming Dictionary
Bernard Dupriez	A Dictionary of Literary Devices
J.A. Cuddon	Dictionary of Literary Terms and Literary Theory
Winthrop Sargeant	The Bhagavad Gita
Bernard Soulie	Tantra Erotic Figures in Indian Art
B.K.S. Iyengar	Light on Pranayama
E. Royston Pike	Encyclopaedia of Religion And Religions
Eugene Saviano	Spanish Idioms
Dagobert D. Runes	Dictionary of Philosophy
Clement Wood	Poet's Handbook
Evan Esar	Esar's Comic Dictionary
Alex Preminger	Princeton Encyclopedia of Poetry and Poetics
Oxford University Press	The Oxford English Dictionary A-B
Diane Arbus	Diane Arbus

55

Carol Clement	Catskills
Frederick Pratson	Guide to Cape Cod
John Willett	Expressionism
Hans Richter	Dada: Art and Anti-Art
El Greco	Every Painting
Harry Mathews	Giandomenico Tiepolo
David Burckhalter	The Seris
Madeleine Johnson	Fire Island 1650s - 1980s
Vladimir Davenport	Tatlin!
Gertrude Stein	Picasso: The Complete Writings
Gregory Battcock and Robert Nickas	Art of Performance

John Berger Success and Failure of Picasso
Betsy Sussler Bomb Interviews
Bob Henning Cornbread Red

56

Marcel Mauss The Gift
Katharine Kuh Break-Up: The Core of Modern Art
Martha Kearns Kathe Kollwitz
The Drawing Center Rajasthani Miniatures
Steve Babson Working Detroit
Jessica Prinz Art Discourse/Discourse In Art
A/D A/D at the Peter Joseph Gallery
Frank and Arthur
  Woodford All Our Yesterdays: A Brief History
    of Detroit
Maurice Sendak Where The Wild Things Are
Karl Marx and
  Friedrich Engels Manifesto of the Communist Party
John Erickson Dada: Performance, Poetry And Art
Max Weber The Protestant Ethic and the Spirit
    of Capitalism

Roger Cardinal
  and Robert Short Surrealism: Permanent Revelation
Rosemary Mayer Pontormo's Diary

57

Miranda Maher 18 Self-portraits, 15 Portraits, 9 Portraits in
    2 Different Forms
Frank Whitford Egon Schiele
Sar Alexandrian Brueghel
Artists Space Warp and Woof: Comfort And Dissent
Hans Hofmann Hans Hofmann Drawings
Rudof Kuenzli New York Dada
Rudy Burckhardt Talking Pictures
Drawing Center Odilon Redon
Barbara Rose Miro in America
Roman Vishniac Polish Jews: Pictorial Record
Gail Levin Edward Hopper
Erica Anderson The World of Albert Schweitzer

Christina Hole   Witchcraft in England
Alan Young   Dada and After

58

The Whitney Museum   Making Mischief: Dada Invades New York
Stephen Foster and   Dada Spectrum; Dialectics of Revolt
  Rudolph Keunzli
Kathe Kollwitz   Diary and Letters of Kathe Kollwitz
Michael Benedikt   The Poetry of Surrealism
Martika Sawin   Surrealism in Exile
Kynaston McShine   Joseph Cornell
I.K. Taimni   The Science of Yoga
Dante   The Divine Comedy
Louise Bourgeois   Louise Bourgeois
Horst Uhr   Masterpieces of German
                          Expressionism
Vincent Van Gogh   Vincent Van Gogh
Colin Wilson   The Outsider
Colin Wilson   A Criminal History of Mankind
Nickie Roberts   Whores in History

59

Sigmund Freud   Dora: An Analysis of a
                          Case of Hysteria
Jules Michelet   Satanism and Witchcraft
Philippe Jullian   The Symbolists
Brian Wallis   Art after Modernism
Bernard Myers   The German Expressionists
Gordon Alexander Craig Europe Since 1914
Museum of Modern Art   The New American Painting
Arthur Emerson   Our Trees: How to Know Them
Christopher Butler   Early Modernism
Dorothea Tanning   Birthday
Patricia Kaplan
  and Susan Manso   Major European Art Movements
Edward Fry   Cubism
Anna Balakian   Surrealism: The Road to the Absolute
Patrick Waldberg   Surrealism

60

Richard Saul Wurman	Access Paris
Musee Picasso	Musee Picasso Visitors Guide
Johanna Drucker	The Century of Artists Books
Jerome Rothenberg and Pierre Joris	Poems for the Millennium Volume 1
Lewis Larmore	Introduction to Photographic Principles
Paul Gardner	Louise Bourgeois
Franz Boas	Primitive Art
John Berger	Ways of Seeing
Francoise Duvivier	Dive
Edgar Preston Richardson	A Short History of Painting in America
Walter Benjamin	Art, Mimesis and the Avant-Garde
Colin Rhodes	Primitivism and Modern Art
Gregory Battcock	Minimal Art
Vasant Lad	The Complete Book of Ayurvedic Home Remedies

61

Michael Ondaatje	The Collected Works of Billy the Kid
Tenney Nathanson	Erased Art
Cole Swenson	Oh
Juliana Spahr	thisconnectionofeveryonewithlungs
Laynie Browne	Pollen Memory
Steve Katz; Cole Swenson	Stolen Stories; Oh
Bobbie Louise Hawkins	One Small Saga
Charles Alexander	Arc of Light
Charles Borkhuis	Mouth of Shadows
David Henderson	The Low East
Michael McClure	Specks
Lewis MacAdams	A Poem for the Dawn of the Terror Years
Laurie Price; Hilda Morley	Except for Memory: To Hold in My Hand
Hilda Morley	To Hold in My Hand

62

Jethro Kloss	Back to Eden
David Hoffmann	New Holistic Herbal
Humbart Santillo	Natural Healing With Herbs

Lila Nachtigall and Joan Rattner Heilman	Estrogen the Facts Can Change Your Life
Rina Nissim	Natural Healing in Gynecology
Jonathan Wright and John Morgenthaler	Natural Hormone Replacement
Unknown	c-f Health Index
Unknown	a-b Health Index
Unknown	g-o Health Index
David Werner	Where There Is No Doctor
Kuhn Rikon	Pressure Cooker Quick Cuisine
Ann Wigmore	The Hippocrates Diet and Health Program
Brian Clement and Theresa Foy Di Geronimo	Living Foods for Optimum Health
Edward Howell	Enzyme Nutrition

63

Stephen Arlin	Raw Power
Jane Brody	Jane Brody's Good Food Book
Eleanor Rosenast	Soup Alive!
Arnold Ehret	Mucusless Diet Healing System
Ann Wigmore	The Sprouting Book
Margaret Grieve	A Modern Herbal, Vol 1
Steve Meyerowitz	Kitchen Garden Cookbook
Vasant Lad	Ayurvedic Cooking for Self-Healing
Rita Romano	Dining in the Raw
Betty Crocker	Betty Crocker Cookbook
William Shurtleff and Akiko Aoyagi	The Book of Miso
W. Y. Evans-Wentz	Tibet's Great Yogi Milarepa
Phylis Balch and James Balch	Prescription for Nutritional Healing
Brenda Coultas	Boy Eye

64

Ed Friedman	Mao & Matisse
Ed Friedman	Drive Through The Blue Cylinders
Charles Cantalupo	Anima/l Wo/man And Other Spirits
Donna Cartelli	Black Mayonnaise
John High	The Sasha Poems

Charlotte Carter	Rhode Island Red
Lewis Warsh	The Origin of the World
Barbara Miller	Yoga Discipline of Freedom
Ray Di Palma	Motion of the Cypher
Alain Robbe-Grillet	For a New Novel
Laura Riding Jackson	Selected Poems
Kent Johnson &	
Craig Paulenich	Beneath A Single Moon
Joshua Taylor	Futurism
Michio Kushi	The Macrobiotic Way

65

Donald Lopez	The Story of Buddhism
Fodor's	City Guide New York
Nasreen Munni Kabir	The Kabir Book
Edward Thomas	Buddhist Scriptures
B.K.S. Iyengar	Light on the Yoga Sutras of Patanjali
Romain Rolland	Life of Rama Krishna
Julianne Dueber	Spanish Vocabulary
Louise Erdrich	Love Medicine
Museum of Modern Art	Fluxus
Lewis Warsh	Touch of the Whip
Idries Shah	Tales of the Dervishes
Hannah Weiner	Words
Bernadette Mayer	Red Book in Three Parts
Lewis Warsh	Reported Missing

66

Lynn Crawford	Simply Separate People
Jeffrey Kripal	Kali's Child
Kim Lyons	Hello Mongolia
Paul Green	A Comparative Daimon
Anne Waldman	
and Lewis Warsh	The Angel Hair Anthology
Tyrone Williams	c.c.
Harryette Mullen	Blues Day
Nina Ishrenko	The Right to Err
Harryette Mullen	Sleeping with the Dictionary
John Keats	Selected Poems and Letters

Lewis Warsh and	
Julie Harrison	Debtor's Prison
Diane di Prima	Recollections of My Life as a Woman
Michael Friedman	Species
Eliza McGrand and	
Brenda Iijima	Shadow Dragging Like a Photographer's Cloth

67

Drew Gardner	Sugar Pill
Kim Hunter	Born on Slow Knives
Richard Kostelanetz	Solos, Tuets, Trois, & Choruses
Jack Kerouac	Satori in Paris
Sunita Mehta	Women for Afghan Women
Elio Schneeman	Along the Rails
Maya Tiwari	Ayurveda: Secrets of Healing
David Frawley	Ayurvedic Healing
David Frawley and	
Vasant Lad	Yoga of Herbs
Michael Murray and	
Joseph Pizzorno	Encyclopedia of Natural Medicine
Devdutt Pattanaik	Devi: The Mother Goddess
Devdutt Pattanaik	Shiva: An Introduction
Devdutt Pattanaik	Vishnu: An Introduction
Thomas Egenes	Introduction to Sanskrit 1

68

Thomas Egenes	Introduction to Sanskrit 2
M. Subbaraya Kamath	Sri Maharshi: A Short Life Sketch
Arthur Osborne	Be Still, It Is The Wind That Sings
Ramana Maharshi	The Collected Works
Lady Wilson	Letters from India
Arthur Osborne	Ramana-Arunachala
Munagala Venkataramiah	Talks with Sri Ramana Maharshi
Heinrich Harrer	Seven Years in Tibet
S. S. Cohen	Guru Ramana
Richard Schiffman	Sri Ramakrishna: A Prophet for the New Age
Dalai Lama	The Way of Freedom

Osho	The Path of Yoga
J. Bruijn	Persian Sufi Poetry
Carl Ernst	Sufism

69

Manil Suri	The Death of Vishnu
Peter Bushyeager	Citadel Luncheonette
Raghubir Singh and	
Joseh Lelyveld	Calcutta
George Ohsawa	Zen Macrobiotics
Kari Edwards	A Day in the Life of P
David Rosenberg	See What You Think
Edward Foster and	
Joseph Donahue	The World in Time and Space
Oliver Sacks	Awakenings
E.M. Forster	A Passage to India
Edward Maisel	Alexander Technique
Pedro de Alcantara	Alexander Technique
Joseph Campbell	Baksheesh & Brahman
Riva Castleman	A Century of Artists Books
Jhumpa Lahiri	Interpreter of Maladies

70

Yuko Tsushimi	Child of Fortune
Yasunari Kawabata	Beauty and Sadness
Gail Tsukiyama	The Samurai's Garden
Ogai Mori	Wild Geese
Sawako Ariyoshi	The River Ki
Ryunosuke Akutagawa	Rashomon and Other Stories
Donald Keene	Modern Japanese Literature
Arundhati Roy	The God of Small Things
Matsuo Basho	The Narrow Road to the Deep North
Thomas Cleary	The Essential Koran
Jacques Jomier	How to Understand Islam
Salman Rushdie and	
Elizabeth West	Mirrorwork
Ananda k. Coomeraswamy	The Dance of Shiva
Khushwant Singh	Train to Pakistan

Ogai Mori	Vita Sexualis
John Esposito	Unholy War
Anne Waldman and	
Andrew Schelling	Songs of the Sons and Daughters of Buddha
Huston Smith	Islam
Ahmed Ali	Twilight in Delhi
Edward Fitzgerald	The Rubaiyat of Omar Khayam
Junichiro Tanizaki	The Makioka Sisters
Karen Armstrong	Islam
Rabindranath Tagore	Gitanjali
Kobo Abe	The Woman in the Dunes
Ruchira Ukerjee	Toad in my Garden
Mowlana Jalaluddin Rumi	The Glance
Yukio Mishima	Confessions of a Mask
Jack Kornfield	Teachings of the Buddha

R. K. Narayan	The Mahabharata
Donald Keene	Anthology of Japanese Literature
Rabindranath Tagore	Songs of Kabir
Haruki Murakami	Sputnik Sweetheart
Muhammad Umar Memon	The Tale of the Old Fisherman
Roland Barthes; Ted Berrigan; S. Foster Damon	A Lover's Discourse; A Certain Slant of Sunlight; A Blake Dictionary
Allen Ginsberg; Mitch Highfill	Howl; Liquid Affairs
Nicole Brossard	Picture Theory
Harry Mathews	Immeasurable Distances
Charles Olson; Toni Morrison	Reading at Berkeley; Jazz
Tyrone Williams; G. Leech; Louis Zukofsky	Callaloo, 22.1; A Linguistic Guide; Complete Short Poetry
Dennis Teichman	Edge to Edge
Douglas Messerli	Language Poetries
James Agee; Alan Young	Let Us Praise These Famous Men; Dada and After

Barbara Henning was born in Detroit, Michigan. She moved to New York City in the early eighties and has recently settled in Tucson, Arizona. She is the author of two novels, the most recent, *You, Me and the Insects,* as well as several books of poetry. *Thirty Miles to Rosebud*—a collection of stories, prose poems and photographs—is forthcoming from Spuyten Duyvil. In the nineties, she was the editor of *Long News: In the Short Century.* She is Professor Emerita from Long Island University in Brooklyn.

UNITED ARTISTS BOOKS

Across the Big Map by Ruth Altmann $12.00
Judyism by Jim Brodey $10.00
Join the Planets by Reed Bye $14.00
The California Papers by Steve Carey $10.00
Personal Effects by Charlotte Carter $8.00
The Fox by Jack Collom $10.00
Columbus Square Journal by William Corbett $10.00
Solution Simulacra by Gloria Frym $14.00
Smoking in the Twilight Bar by Barbara Henning $8.00
Love Makes Thinking Dark by Barbara Henning $10.00
My Autobiography by Barbara Henning $14.00
Liquid Affairs by Mitch Highfill $10.00
Poems for the Whole Family by Daniel Krakauer $8.00
Head by Bill Kushner $8.00
Love Uncut by Bill Kushner $10.00
That April by Bill Kushner $12.00
One at a Time by Gary Lenhart $10.00
Another Smashed Pinecone by Bernadette Mayer $10.00
Red Book in Three Parts by Bernadette Mayer $8.00
Something to Hold On To by Dennis Moritz $8.00
Songs for the Unborn Second Baby by Alice Notley $16.00
Fool Consciousness by Liam O'Gallagher $8.00
Cleaning Up New York by Bob Rosenthal $10.00
Political Conditions/Physical States by Tom Savage $10.00
In the Heart of the Empire by Harris Schiff $8.00
Along the Rails by Elio Schneeman $10.00
Continuity Girl by Chris Tysh $12.00
Echolalia by George Tysh $10.00
Selected Poems by Charlie Vermont $8.00
Blue Mosque by Anne Waldman $10.00
The Maharajah's Son by Lewis Warsh $12.00
Information from the Surface of Venus by Lewis Warsh $12.00
Reported Missing by Lewis Warsh $8.00
Clairvoyant Journal by Hannah Weiner $14.00
The Fast by Hannah Weiner $10.00

United Artists Books
114 W. 16th Street, 5C
New York, NY 10011
lwarsh@mindspring.com
www.unitedartists.com

Small Press Distribution
1341 Seventh St.
Berkeley, CA 94710
www.spdbooks.org